Jack Tworkov

Jack Tworkov Fifteen Years of Painting

The Solomon R. Guggenheim Museum, New York

This exhibition is supported by a grant from the National Endowment for the Arts, a Federal Agency

Published by The Solomon R. Guggenheim Foundation, New York, 1982

ISBN: 0-89207-033-1

Library of Congress Card Catalog Number: 81-85808

Cover: cat. no. 26. *Q3-78-#3*. 1978

Lenders to the Exhibition

Jacqueline and Myron Blank, Des Moines, Iowa

Estate of Dr. Louis L. Heyn

I.B.M. Corporation, New York

Dr. and Mrs. Leroy Lavine

Mr. and Mrs. I. M. Pei

Beatrice Perry, New York

Jacob Schulman, Gloversville, New York

Jack Tworkov

The Cleveland Museum of Art

The Solomon R. Guggenheim Museum, New York

San Francisco Museum of Modern Art

Nancy Hoffman Gallery, New York

Preface and Acknowledgements

The mature work of Jack Tworkov clearly divides into two components that at first glance appear remote from, if not incompatible with, each other: his "hot" gestural painting of the 1950s and early 1960s and his "cool" measured work of subsequent years, to use the designations supplied by Andrew Forge in the essay that follows in this catalogue. Since this exhibition is not conceived as a full retrospective but as a survey of Tworkov's painting from the last fifteen years, only his later phase is presented here. The selection was so restricted in full agreement with the artist in order to stress the autonomy of the direction he has pursued since 1966. Obviously, an emphasis of this kind is not gained without a concomitant loss—in this instance, the loss of that other Tworkov whose spontaneous Abstract Expressionist canvases of the earlier years assured him a place of honor among the first generation of artists who created the new American painting in the wake of World War II.

In an exhibition concerned with Tworkov's lifework, the absence of the production of the fifties and the first half of the sixties would be unthinkable, for as Andrew Forge's essay makes plain, the two Tworkovs, ultimately comprehensible as one, stand to each other in a dialectic relationship that is close to the central meaning of his art. Our purpose, however, is to isolate Tworkov's classic strain and to bring before the viewer works indicative of the range and the fullness of this geometric mode.

I wish to thank Linda Shearer, who, as Guest Curator of this exhibition, worked closely with the artist in selecting the paintings on display. Her sensitivity and acumen are reflected in the choices made. The exhibition and the accompanying catalogue are supported by the National Endowment for the Arts— the Federal Agency that has enabled the Guggenheim Museum and other cultural institutions throughout the United States to maintain significant levels of production.

Thomas M. Messer, *Director*
The Solomon R. Guggenheim Foundation

The successful realization of this exhibition and catalogue were made possible through the commitment of many individuals. I am, above all, indebted to Jack Tworkov, who has enthusiastically participated in every aspect of the undertaking. I am grateful, too, for the unfailing support of Wally Tworkov, the artist's wife. Thanks are due to Nancy Hoffman, the artist's dealer, and her staff, whose assistance with both exhibition and publication has been invaluable. Andrew Forge, long the artist's friend and admirer, has enriched the catalogue with his cogent essay. I gratefully acknowledge the efforts and dedication of numerous members of the Guggenheim Museum staff. In particular, my sincerest thanks are extended to Susan B. Hirschfeld, Exhibitions Coordinator, for her indispensable contributions to all phases of the exhibition as well as the catalogue. I am also grateful to Carol Fuerstein, Editor, for her skillful editing of the publication and handling of its production, and to Cynthia Clark, Editorial Assistant, for her careful help with the catalogue. Finally, I would like to thank the lenders, without whom this exhibition could not have taken place.

Linda Shearer

The Knight and the Barrier

by Andrew Forge

Jack Tworkov has never learned to take his work for granted, nor, one might add, his very existence. The habit of asking questions is ingrained. For the last fifteen years or so his painting has been based on more or less predetermined systems of construction, a direction he took in reaction to the cul-de-sac that faced him and many of his Abstract Expressionist colleagues. But "I have misgivings, worries about my present work," he wrote only a year ago. "It's true, system does not exclude spontaneity and fresh invention, but it does include an element of the mechanical, the predictable. My earlier work, although it tended to resolve itself into a predictable style . . . nevertheless . . . was preceded at least at the start, by a *void*, by the absence of any ascertainable direction. In contrast, the present paintings begin with exact drawings, almost equivalent to an architect's drawing, and the painting follows the exact surface divisions, proportions and the arrived shapes and forms. Only the actual painting, the work with the brush, and the development of the color and surface is left to the spontaneous decision of the moment."

How to recover a broader spontaneity, he asks himself in this irritable self-critique, written in a sketchbook on his knee in a train. None of his attempts, his tentative studies, have satisfied him. On the contrary, they have seemed less "inspired" than the paintings based on systems.

So the round goes on. Few artists of his stature have felt so acutely the contradictions implicit in being a painter caught between the inner necessities of the studio and the dubious external relationships given in our benighted time. He has an intense longing for content and for meaningful links between what he is doing in the studio and the world outside. This longing is expressed repeatedly in conversation, in writing, in his teaching. He is looking for something more than the recognition of a gallery-going public, and at the back of all his questioning of his own studio procedures one senses a larger questioning, addressed to the culture, to the institutions of art, to the sense of self and of community. And out of that larger question there comes an acknowledgement of frailty and of dependence on painting as a continual remaking of the self. "I am not ashamed to confess that I've seen my work . . . not merely as 'a way of life' but as a way to save my life."

It has been a long working life. Born with the century, Tworkov first showed in the late twenties. He was an easel painter on the Project. After the war he saw, was part of, the massing and breaking of that great wave of energies that produced the School of New York, now dispersed. By temperament he is a man of balance and of conscience—but one for whom the activity of painting is a personal necessity, unreasonable and amoral though it is.

He has never learned to resolve this contradiction nor to ignore the pain of it. An inveterate journal-keeper, his writing is like an extended critique of himself and his times in which the most awkward questions are nagged at compulsively over the years. But the habit of asking questions is itself only another reminder of the dichotomies between art and life: "I find I can only work without asking myself questions, without ideas. If I start thinking about meaning—I can only ask questions . . . but I cannot come up with answers that will materially change my work or push it into well-supported directions. . . ."

Far too fastidious ever to fall into bohemian clichés of creativity, still he has to work with a sense of contradiction between the wordless involvements of the studio and the dialect of "real life." It is not an easy position to hold. Yet he demands a justification for it, something beyond the inflated value the West has put on art. The *culte de moi* is not enough. "Art can pollute our life as much as technology can pollute our air and water." Modern art, he tells himself in a note of quiet fury, is radical, nihilistic and pessimistic for "it sees no hope in societal values—individual life is without relation to common values—is for itself by itself. This is misery—but where is the way out?"

It is his fate to contradict, to be more convinced by contradiction itself than by its poles: "I have to believe in an art that does not strive for any overt significance or meaning; an art that does not set out to reflect the world or life. . . ."; but at other times the pain is not to be dispersed with stoicism and his sense of alienation from the present and exile from a richer imagined past is as vivid as it has ever been: "I nevertheless feel some inner deprivation, some sorrowful regret that my art is not more explicitly some expression of existence outside and beyond myself. . . ."

Writing a few years ago about his use of geometry, I remarked, "Obviously Tworkov is not using it symbolically as it was used in the Christian-Neoplatonic tradition. Nor is he using it as an aesthetic gloss, a guide to pictorial decorum, as it was its fate to be used in the academies. . . . His love for it is evident, yet he makes no special claim for it either as an aesthetic canon nor as the vehicle for ideas outside painting." And I concluded, "It is utterly neutral, and one supposes that it is precisely this neutrality, this self-evident consistency that is valuable to him. He puts us all on the same level in front of these canvases, as if we were all cousins to that slave of Socrates who . . . was called in to prove the self-evident truth of a geometrical theorem."

I now feel this was too abrupt. For one thing, no describable feature of any painting of quality is without symbolic value. There is more to be said about the values that accrue to Tworkov's use of geometry, perhaps best by comparing one of his earlier, gestural paintings, and one of his geometrical ones of about twelve years later. The main difference between them can be expressed in terms of a dramatic contrast of *distance.* It is worth trying to describe the features that contribute to this feeling.

Barrier Series No. 5 of 1963 (fig. 1), a canvas of about five feet by six and a half, is divided vertically into four roughly drawn sections. They lean somewhat to the right. One senses that the section at the far right is leaning slightly out of the picture and that the section at the far left is leaning into it from the outside: there is less of it to be seen than of the others. The painting as a whole has the aspect of a piece or detail of something much larger than itself, a world of long, leaning columns made of flame-like brushstrokes vigorously licking up and down. The colors with which these columns are brushed move from the left from a cold brownish gray through which one can see glints of blue, to a rich warm brown (the second column) to a powerful orange-red, not far from scarlet, the color of the two columns on the right. Crossing over these

columns, silhouetted in front of them, are three thick bluish black lines that
form a fragment of a grid, somewhat bent to the right. A fourth line is buried in
the interior of the painting. It runs slanting across the canvas and is visible in
the gaps between the long color strokes which envelop it. These strokes—the
fiery orange and the brown—make a vigorous advance: they threaten to en-
gulf the dark lines on the surface, licking over them here and there, breaking
into their edges.

It is almost impossible to describe the painting without engaging in ani-
mistic fantasies: it seems natural to describe the color as hot, fiery, smoulder-
ing; the brushstrokes as flaming. From this it is a short step to seeing the
leaning and bending of the edges of forms as a reaction to the "heat" of the
color, a twisting and buckling as of timbers or girders in intense heat.

There is of course another line to be followed out—although it is writing
that insists on this sequential extension, not the painting. This is the interpre-
tation of the painting as the result of studio activity; to read the brushstrokes
as gestures, to enter into the athletic, improvisatory history of their making.
From this point of view we are drawn into an awesome display of energy. We
can sense the shaping of the whole picture by the action of arm and hand.
The way that almost every feature leans over to the right is like a right-handed
hatching on an enormous scale, a natural orientation of gesture which has
become an ordering of the whole surface.

All these features seen in simultaneous conjunction serve to bring the
picture into very close range. A hot, blazing fragment made visible to us by a
palpably physical action, we cannot gain distance from it on any terms. The
relation between action and the resulting form is one to one. To engage with
the picture at all is to be very close to it indeed.

A painting called *Knight Series OC #3* of 1975 (fig. 2) contrasts with
Barrier in almost every nameable aspect. Seven and a half feet tall, just over
six feet wide, it is divided into a regular grid of one hundred and twenty
squares. The square of the shorter side of the canvas, that is the lower ten

ranks of ten squares, provides the field for a smaller square, eight by eight, the divisions of a chessboard. Within this there is contained a more complex geometrical figure. In describing these features to one's self, it seems natural to move from the whole canvas to the way it is divided, from the regular grid of squares to the larger square, the "chessboard." Each stage of the description is complete in itself: it does not overlap with another stage.

The construction lines are plainly visible, a delicate but firm framework for whatever else is to be seen in the painting. The divisions are linear but in most cases reinforced by changes in color. The outer margin of the painting is the most densely brushed, a cool pewter gray. The field of the chessboard is a paler blue-gray. The geometrical figure within the chessboard is divided into different areas of white (the surface of the canvas), pale yellow and a warmer gray which in certain areas crosses the yellow. All these colors are applied with a small, uniformly repeated up-and-down stroke worked out in neat rows, four deep to the square. This repeated stroke, which resembles nothing so much as the kind of copybook exercise that used to be given to children when they were being taught to write, is small enough to provide a completely unified surface, open enough to be transparent and vigorous enough to set up a faint background vibration. Where one layer of color is brushed over another, as in the outer margin of the picture, the surface is

fig. 2
Knight Series OC #3.   1975
Oil on canvas
Courtesy Nancy Hoffman Gallery,
New York

A diagonal grid is formed by dividing the square into three, five and eight segments (left) and connecting all peripheral points to one another (right). Each resulting line is the diagonal of a rectangle.

Diagram by the artist, fall 1981

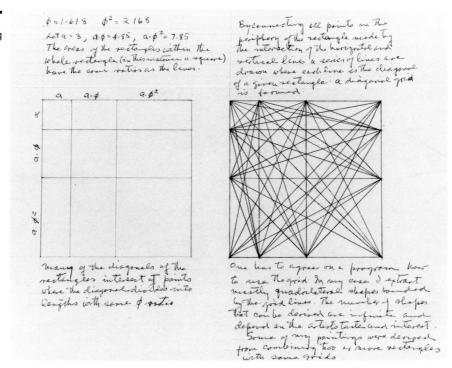

denser but takes on a more complex tonality, a kind of luster. None of these changes interferes with the grid structures for which the color serves as an infilling, like a dense script filling the pages of a book.

The figure within the chessboard is different from anything else in the picture. The title directs our attention to the Knight's move in chess, and in fact it is this move of two squares along and one to the side which determines the drawing of the whole figure. Each move is marked by a dot, starting from the Knight's proper square on the top rank of the board, moving across to KR4, then on KB1 on the opposite side, zigzagging back, crossing his tracks but never resting on a square he had rested on before. His journey stops when he arrives at Q1 on his own side. What this imaginary knight has done is to "draw" a variety of overlapping squares, triangles and polygons. His resting places are marked and joined with a ruled line. Four shapes are chosen to be colored—a tilted square which is to be yellow, and two smaller rectangles and a more complicated figure with seven sides which takes the darker gray. The rest is left white.

The figure facing us thus offers a choice of two distinct readings: we can see it as a group of overlapping planes placed simultaneously in front of us, or we can see it as a linear path, to be followed sequentially (in either direction) from start to finish. To do this is to engage in the making of the figure, to follow each move as a decision and, in the end, to ponder decisions about which area is to be colored and when to end the game. Neither reading is definitive, obviously, nor do they merge with each other. They are discrete, cannot be "seen" at the same time, although the knowledge or memory of the alternative will be present in our minds as we engage in one or the other reading.

It is clear from this comparison that the two paintings bring out contrasting modes of thought and feeling, contrasting states of awareness. It is not just that the paintings *look* different; they stand for different mental operations and different ways of apprehending the world.

Barrier leads to sensations of closeness, an almost overwhelming sense of melting, of being drawn into a fiery opening, into something much larger, something boundless and terrible. *Knight*, cool and pale in tonality, is distanced, contained, bounded. Its margins are calmly stated and seem to affirm the boundaries between ourselves and the picture, and indeed the gap across which we read it.

Our reading of *Barrier* happens explosively and chaotically. The picture seems to pour in upon us at once. One reading of it fuses with another. The picture takes on many identities which glide back and forth like identities in a dream which are nonetheless vivid for being ambivalent. It is as though moments of time were opened up to simultaneous experience. Our reading of *Knight,* on the other hand, happens sequentially; we move from feature to feature, from whole to part, from division to subdivision. It is a cumulative reading in which each stage seems to be experienced, told over, in an orderly progression. This quality is epitomized in the final engagement with the knight's move which is only completely understood when it has been run to its conclusion as a sequence in time.

What is to be made of the comparisons I have drawn here? The two phases of Tworkov's painting seem to cover an immense span of human experience. The meaning of any painter's work is cumulative. I find it impossible to disassociate Tworkov's geometric painting from what has gone before. Both phases complement each other in spite of their apparently irreconcilable tenors. Each achieves its fullness of meaning in the other's light, and one suspects that the argument has in fact never been broken off.

Was the change to geometrics the result of a blinding conversion? Surely not. We need to be able to see the two phases of his work as opposing factors in his own continuing questions, even if one of them has, for a season or a decade, been argued into silence. Of course the times had their impact. His move from "hot" gestural painting to "cool" measured painting paralleled the moves that were being made by younger painters in the early sixties, a reaction to the clichés of Abstract Expressionism. It was part of a general revulsion against the condition of a whole school that was trapped sentimentally in its own myth about itself. This was perhaps his surface reason, his message and critique aimed at his generation.

But there were compelling private reasons. "I was eager to experiment," he told Marcia Tucker in an interview, "I wasn't content to form a style and stay with it. Then I found that in order to experiment, *I had to have some constant that I could fasten on to,* at least some elements, certain divisions of the canvas, for instance, that I could measure and repeat. Therefore I could take the same kind of structure and paint it differently." (My italics)

The improvisation of the earlier mode, starting with a void, ends in a predictable "style" in which the freedom to experiment is lacking. Warmth, proximity, an overwhelming and absorbing presence could, with luck on his side, be won from the engagement with paint and the vast physical demands of the canvas. A show of aggression, a masterful and omnipotent command, could with luck on his side, bring about a strong concrete symbol, a form that looked back at him, that returned his energy and angry drive, a chunk of the world bitten off, annexed to himself. The mood was insistently repetitive; the canvas a mirror in which only one likeness was returned. But in order to experiment, that is, to essay, to attempt, to investigate, to rifle the unknown, to experience freshness and novelty—that is, to pass into a more evolved relationship with the world—he had to find "a constant" that he could "fasten on to" and it had to be something that he could "measure and repeat." What an extraordinary paradox!

The point is that this constant was *out there*. Geometry provided a structure whose existence could be acknowledged outside of himself. It was there whenever he wanted it. It could be lost, but found again. It made no demands —yet its laws were as inexorable as they were self-evident. He could only use it in an attitude of respect for it: a line is either straight or not; two lines either meet or do not.

In a moving note Tworkov has written, "The hope that art reveals the whole man is frustrated—at best we show bits and pieces of ourselves often ambiguous as if they didn't belong to the same person. And indeed we make our appearances under different masks, masks sometimes imposed on us by our modesty—more often by hypocrisy. Art becomes a formal game, a civilized dance—unfortunately." We catch here something utterly characteristic of him, a kind of debonair despair, a hint of bitter pain behind the worldly demeanor. His despair is pointed at the world, at the horror of things as they really are. He cannot comfort himself, least of all by the fictional comforts of art. Corrupt contemporary usages of art turn him off. At the same time, he is tied to art and cannot relinquish its magic.

To return one more time to the comparison of *Barrier* and *Knight.* I find it obvious that the earlier work calls up a more primitive awareness, a magical domain that only art allows us to enter at will in which boundaries are fused and everything is subject to manipulation. Time, space, distinctions between here and there have all run together in a single flow of energy. *Knight* declares an opposite extreme. In its world, things stand at a distance, and in their freestandingness do not answer to the same kind of omnipotent manipulation. We could say that it tokens a view of reality that acknowledges the existence of the outside world, the reality of time and space, and, with the dropping of omnipotence, of death. His energy can ebb and flow. He can turn his back on the painting: it will still be there when he returns. "Art is the metropolis of symbolic manifestation," Adrian Stokes has written. "We practice therein the rites of symbolism. Consequently, we may practice there . . . every mode of perception." In contemplating side by side these two phases of Tworkov's painting, it seems to me that we are drawn into two universal modes of perception, the storming unities of infancy, its rages and enveloping comforts—and the anxious responsibility of later experience with its mature recognition of a freestanding reality with its acceptance of potential loss.

I have called one phase of Tworkov's painting hot and the other cool and have stressed the contrast between them. It is a feature of the very greatest art that it sets the stage for traffic between these two extremes. Tworkov's reiteration of the limits and even poverty of today's art perhaps reflects an intuition that such traffic is for us scarcely possible. Modern art has insisted on purity, on unity of purpose, on reduction even at the risk of poverty. By his own testimony he has not found the elbow room he needed for his generous dialectic. But I would insist that there is compelling meaning in the single notes that he has been forced to sing. I have no difficulty in reading his works as parables, rich in reference to our uneasy place in the world.

Works in the Exhibition

1. *Trace.*   1966
   Oil on canvas, 50 x 69″
   Lent by the artist, courtesy Nancy
   Hoffman Gallery, New York

2. *Follower I.* 1967
   Oil on canvas, 50 x 69″
   Collection of the artist

3. *Note.* 1968
Oil on linen, 80 x 70″
Collection Mr. and Mrs. I. M. Pei

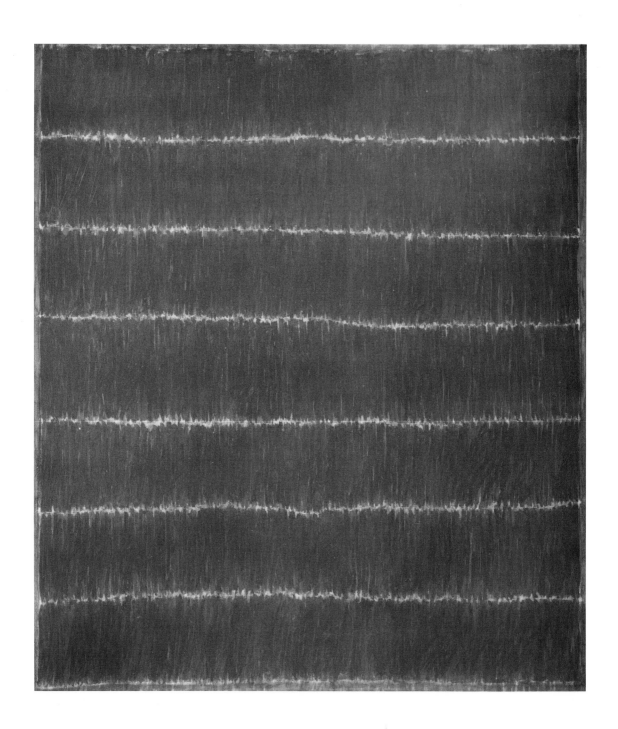

5. *Jag (SP-69-#4).* 1969
   Oil on linen, 80 x 70″
   Lent by the artist, courtesy Nancy
   Hoffman Gallery, New York

6.   *Bloomfield.*   1969
     Oil on canvas, 80 x 70″
     Collection Jacob Schulman, Glovers-
     ville, New York

7. *Idling III.* 1970
   Oil on linen, 80 x 70″
   Collection San Francisco Museum of
   Modern Art, Gift of the artist

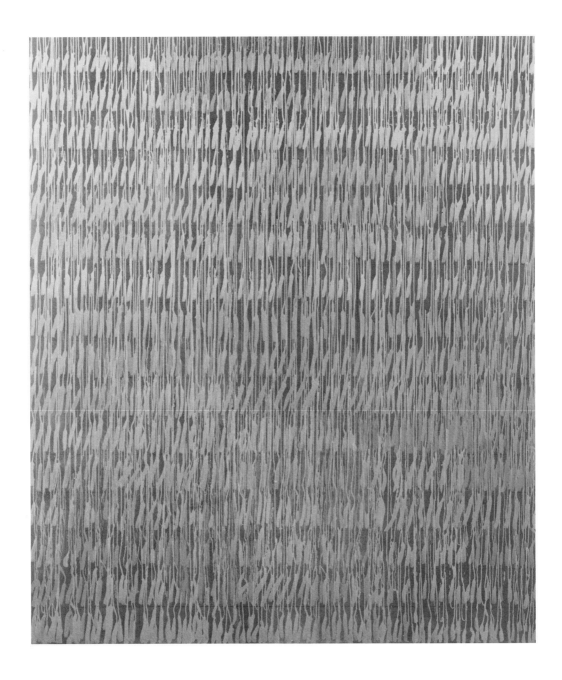

8. *Crossfield III (WNY-70-3).*   1970
Oil on linen, 80 x 96″
Lent by the artist, courtesy Nancy
Hoffman Gallery, New York

9. *Pyramid (Q3-71-3).* 1971
   Oil on linen, 72 x 72″
   Lent by the artist, courtesy Nancy
   Hoffman Gallery, New York

10. *Diptych #1.* 1971
   Oil on linen, two panels, each
   85 x 60″
   Lent by the artist, courtesy Nancy
   Hoffman Gallery, New York

11. *Bin (NY-Q1-72-3).*   1971-72
     Oil on canvas, 80 x 80″
     Lent by the artist, courtesy Nancy
     Hoffman Gallery, New York

12. *Diptych II.* 1972
Oil on canvas, two panels, each
76 x 76"
Collection The Solomon R. Guggen-
heim Museum, New York. Purchased
with the aid of funds from the
National Endowment for the Arts in
Washington, D.C., a Federal Agency;
matching funds contributed by Mrs.
Leo Simon, New York, 1972

13. *Tilt.* 1972
    Oil on canvas, 80 x 70″
    Lent by the artist, courtesy Nancy
    Hoffman Gallery, New York

14. *P 73 #2.* 1973
Oil on canvas, 72 x 72"
Collection Jacqueline and Myron
Blank, Des Moines, Iowa

15. *P 73 #7.*   1973
     Oil on canvas, 93 x 127"
     Lent by the artist, courtesy Nancy
     Hoffman Gallery, New York

16. *Q3-74-#2.* 1974
Oil on canvas, 72 x 72″
Lent by the artist, courtesy Nancy
Hoffman Gallery, New York

17. *Q3-74-#5* 1974
Oil on canvas, 72 x 72″
Lent by the artist, courtesy Nancy
Hoffman Gallery, New York

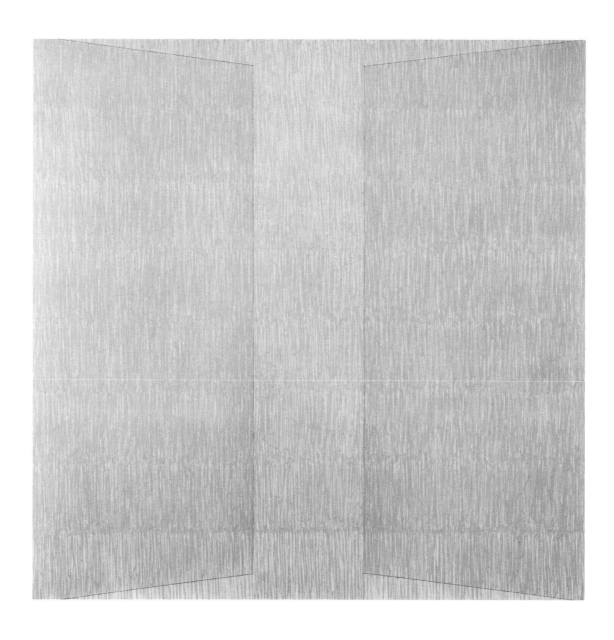

18. *Three-Five-Eight #2 (Q3-75-#7).*
     1975
     Oil on canvas, 80 x 80″
     Lent by the artist, courtesy Nancy
     Hoffman Gallery, New York

19. *Knight Series OC #1 (Q3-75-#2).*
1975
Oil on canvas, 90 x 75″
Collection The Cleveland Museum of
Art, purchased with a grant from the
National Endowment for the Arts and
matched gifts from members of The
Cleveland Society for Contemporary
Art

20. *Triptych Q3-75 #1.* 1975
Oil on canvas, three panels, total
72 x 216″
Lent by the artist, courtesy Nancy
Hoffman Gallery, New York

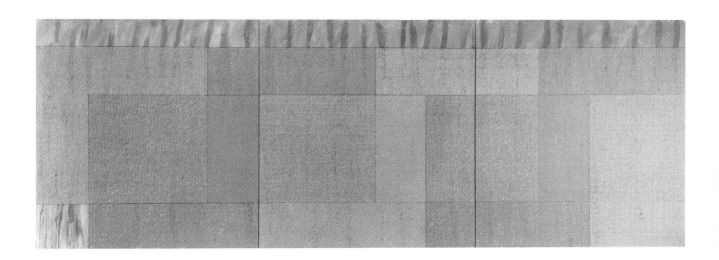

21. *Knight Series #5 (Q3-76-#6).*
    1976
    Oil on canvas, 90 x 75″
    Lent by the artist, courtesy Nancy
    Hoffman Gallery, New York

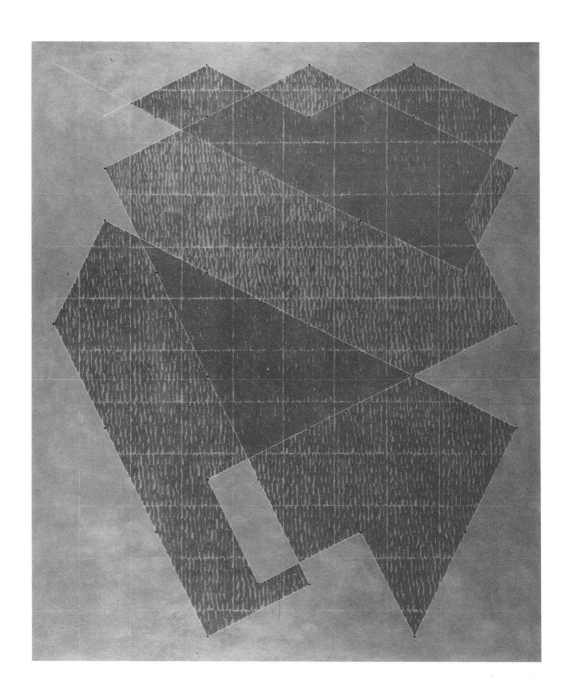

22. *Airgame (Q2-76-#3).* 1976
Oil on canvas, 80 x 140″
Lent by the artist, courtesy Nancy
Hoffman Gallery, New York

23. *Olympia (Q3-76-#2).* 1976
Oil on canvas, 65 x 114"
Lent by the artist, courtesy Nancy
Hoffman Gallery, New York

24. *Hymnos (Q3-76-#3).*   1976
Oil on canvas, 55½ x 96″
Collection Estate of Dr. Louis L. Heyn

25. *Q3-78-#1.* 1978
Oil on canvas, 36 x 108"
Lent by the artist, courtesy Nancy
Hoffman Gallery, New York

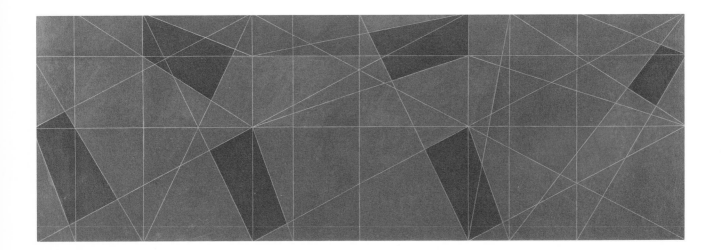

26. *Q3-78-#3.* 1978
Oil on canvas, 54 x 54"
Lent by the artist, courtesy Nancy
Hoffman Gallery, New York

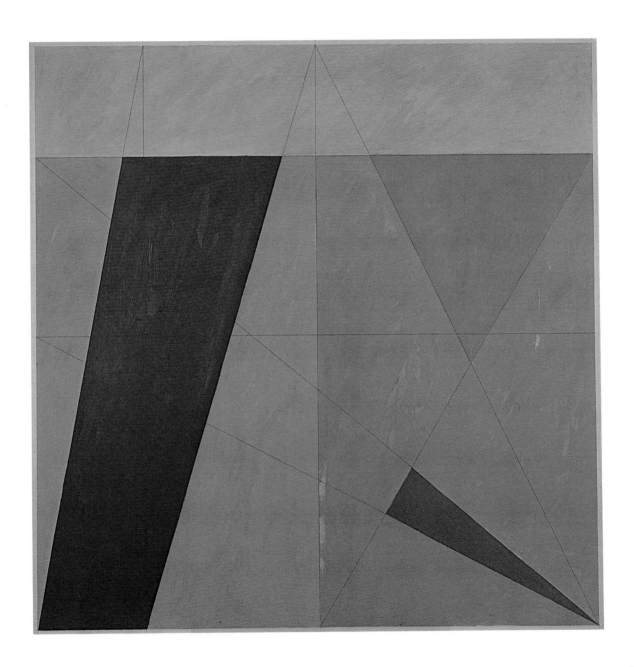

27. *Alternative V (OC-Q1-78).* 1978
     Oil on canvas, 54 x 54″
     Collection Jacob Schulman, Glovers-
     ville, New York

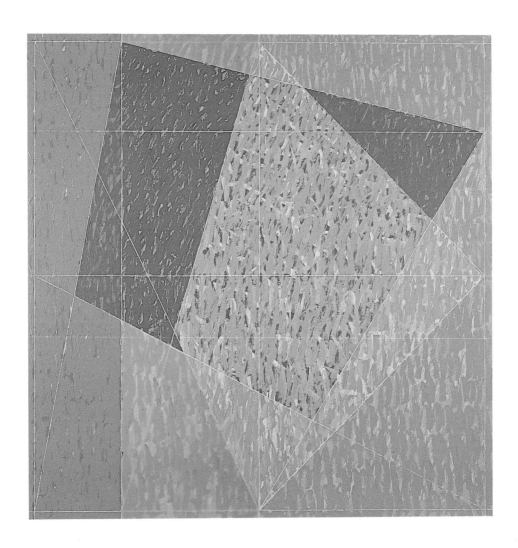

28. *Alternative VIII.* 1978
     Oil on canvas, 54 x 54"
     Lent by the artist, courtesy Nancy
     Hoffman Gallery, New York

29. *Alternative IX.* 1978
Oil on canvas, 72 x 72″
Lent by the artist, courtesy Nancy
Hoffman Gallery, New York

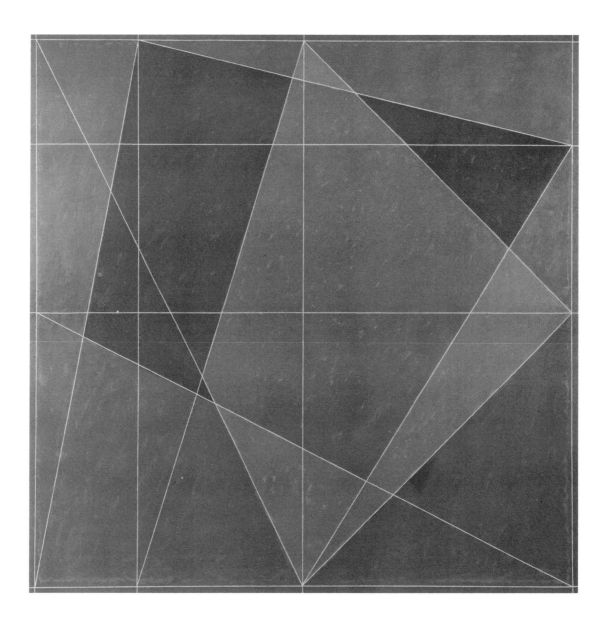

30. *Indian Red Series #1.* 1979
Oil on canvas, 72 x 72"
Lent by the artist, courtesy Nancy
Hoffman Gallery, New York

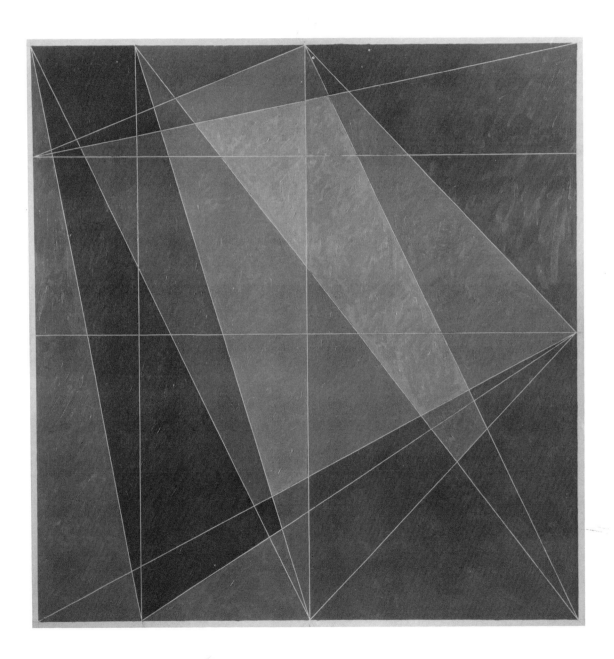

31. *Indian Red Series #2.*   1979
Oil on canvas, 72 x 72"
Lent by the artist, courtesy Nancy
Hoffman Gallery, New York

32. *Indian Red Series #4.*   1979
     Oil on canvas, 72 x 72″
     Lent by the artist, courtesy Nancy
     Hoffman Gallery, New York

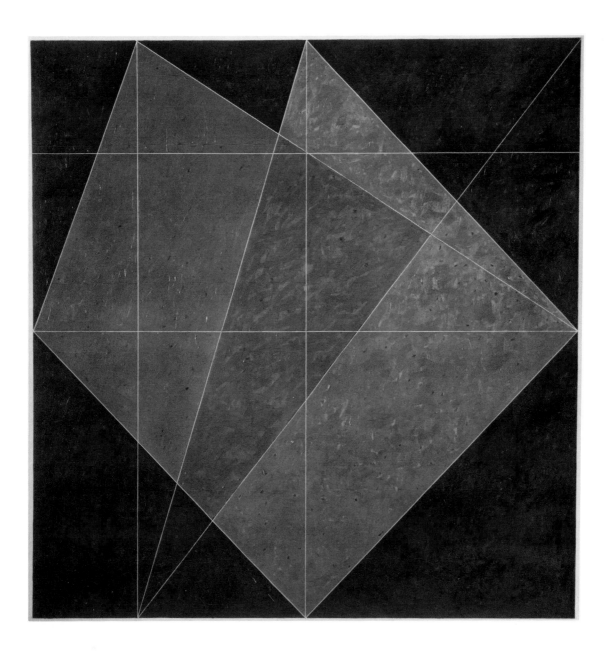

33. *The Exes.* 1980
     Oil on canvas, 57 x 84½″
     Lent by the artist, courtesy Nancy
     Hoffman Gallery, New York

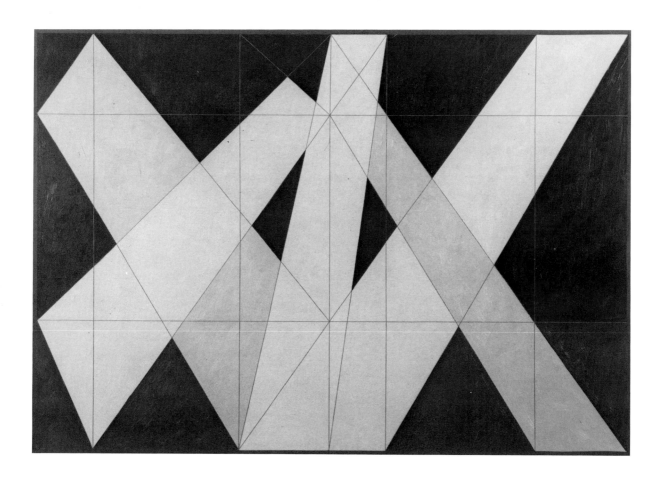

34. *Circle in a Square II (Q4-80-OC-#3).*
    1980
    Oil on canvas, 31½ x 31½"
    Lent by the artist, courtesy Nancy
    Hoffman Gallery, New York

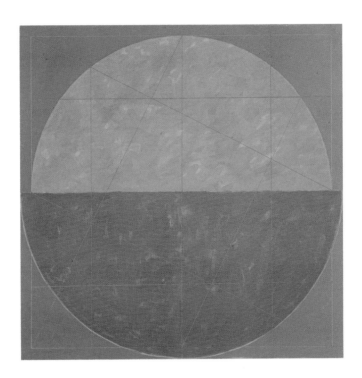

35. *Circle in a Square IV (Q4-80-OC-#9).*
1980
Oil on canvas, 48 x 45″
Lent by the artist, courtesy Nancy
Hoffman Gallery, New York

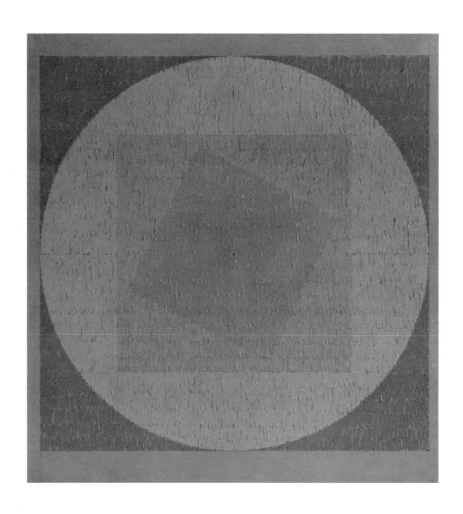

36. *Progressions I (Q1-80-#2).* 1980
Acrylic on canvas, 36 x 108″
Collection I.B.M. Corporation,
New York

37. *Progressions II (Q1-80-#2).* 1980
Oil on canvas, 36 x 108″
Lent by the artist, courtesy Nancy
Hoffman Gallery, New York

38. *Expansion and Contraction of the
    Square I.* 1980
    Oil on canvas, 25½ x 79″
    Lent by the artist, courtesy Nancy
    Hoffman Gallery, New York

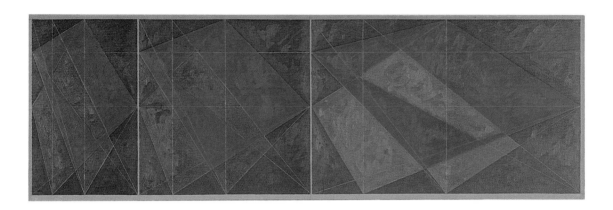

39. *Expansion and Contraction of the
    Square II.*   1980
    Oil on canvas, 26 x 78″
    Collection Dr. and Mrs. Leroy Lavine

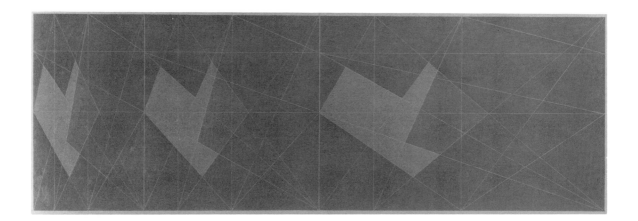

40. *Roman IX.* 1981
Oil on canvas, 95 x 50"
Lent by the artist, courtesy Nancy
Hoffman Gallery, New York

41. *Roman XI.*   1981
Oil on canvas, 100 x 54″
Lent by the artist, courtesy Nancy
Hoffman Gallery, New York

42. *Q.2-O.O.K.-#2*
Progression Series #4.   1980
Oil on kindura paper, 12½ x 32½″
Courtesy Nancy Hoffman Gallery,
New York

43. *O.O.P.-#1-Q.3-80.*   1980
Oil on paper, 14 x 17″
Courtesy Nancy Hoffman Gallery,
New York

44. *Q.3-81-O.P. #2.*   July 26, 1981
Oil on paper, 14 x 14″
Private Collection, New York

45. *Q.3-81-O.P. #6.*   1981
Oil on paper, 18 x 23″
Courtesy Nancy Hoffman Gallery,
New York

46. *Q.3-81-O.P. #11.*   1981
Oil on paper, 15 x 22″
Courtesy Nancy Hoffman Gallery,
New York

47. *Q.4-81-O.P. #2.*   1981
Oil on paper, 22 x 30″
Courtesy Nancy Hoffman Gallery,
New York

Chronology

by Susan B. Hirschfeld

1900
August 15
Born in Biala, Poland.

1913
Emigrates to United States and settles in New York City. Subsequently attends New York public schools; takes drawing class at Stuyvesant High School.

1920-23
Majors in English at Columbia University, New York. Begins association with Lee Gatch.

1923
First of many summers in Provincetown, Massachusetts.

1923-25
Studies at National Academy of Design, New York, with Ivan D. Olinsky and Charles Hawthorne.

1924
In Provincetown studies with Ross Moffett, who introduces him to Karl Knaths.

1925-26
Studies at Art Students League, New York, with Guy Pène du Bois and Boardman Robinson.

1928
Becomes United States citizen.

1929
Spends year painting in Provincetown. Exhibits with Société Anonyme, New York. Paints figures, still lifes and landscapes in this period; influence of Cézanne appears, continues into next decade.

1933
Brief trip to Europe, first since emigration to America.

1934
Participates in United States Treasury Department's Public Works of Art Project.

1935-41
Employed in easel division of WPA Federal Art Project in New York; friendship with Willem de Kooning begins while both are working on Project.

1940
First one-man exhibition at A.C.A. Gallery, New York.

1942-45
Stops painting to work in war industry as tool designer.

1945
Resumes painting; begins to experiment with abstraction.

Self Portrait. January 31, 1982
Pencil on paper
Courtesy of the artist

1947-54
Annual one-man exhibitions at Charles Egan Gallery, New York.

1948
One-man exhibition at The Baltimore Museum of Art.

1948-51
Summers
Teaches at American University, Washington, D.C.

1950s
Develops mature Abstract Expressionist style; spontaneous flame-like brushstrokes define grid.

1952
Green Landscape, 1949, acquired by The Baltimore Museum of Art, his first museum purchase.
July
Visiting Artist, Black Mountain College, Black Mountain, North Carolina.

1954, 55
Summers
Teaches at Indiana University, Bloomington.

1954
Fall
Teaches at University of Mississippi, Oxford.

1955-58
Teaches life drawing at Pratt Institute, Brooklyn.

1957
One-man exhibition at Walker Art Center, Minneapolis.
Winter
Teaches at University of Minnesota, Minneapolis.

1962
Spring
Visiting Artist, School of Art and Architecture, Yale University, New Haven.

1963
Awarded first William A. Clark Prize accompanied by Corcoran Gold Medal, *28th Biennial Exhibition of American Painting,* Corcoran Gallery of Art, Washington, D.C. Appointed Chairman of Art Department, School of Art and Architecture, Yale University; serves in this capacity until 1969. Receives M.F.A. In Privatum, Yale University.

1964
Whitney Museum of American Art, New York, mounts retrospective of his work, which subsequently travels in United States.

mid-1960s
Geometric emphasis emerges; gesture becomes increasingly controlled, dark grays and subdued pastels are used.

1969
William C. Leffingwell Professor of Painting, Emeritus, Yale University.

1970s
Geometric structure of works based on diagonals and abutting angles; strong color reintroduced.

1970
Receives John Simon Guggenheim Foundation Fellowship.

1971
Doctor of Fine Arts, Maryland Institute of Art, Baltimore. One-man exhibition at Whitney Museum of American Art, New York.

1972
Doctor of Humane Letters, Columbia University. Artist-in-Residence, American Academy, Rome.

1973
Winter
Artist-in-Residence, Dartmouth College, Hanover, New Hampshire.
Spring'
Visiting Artist, Columbia University.

1974
Visiting Critic, Royal College of Art, London. Receives Painter of the Year Award, Skowhegan School of Art, Maine. Begins to show at Nancy Hoffman Gallery, New York.

1975
Visiting Artist, Cooper Union School of Art, New York, and New York Studio School.

1976
Winter
Visiting Artist, University of California, Santa Barbara.

1979
Winter
Visiting Artist, California State College, Long Beach. Honorary Degree, Rhode Island School of Design, Providence. One-man exhibition mounted by Third Eye Centre, Glasgow; subsequently travels in Great Britain.

1981
Elected member American Academy and Institute of Arts and Letters.
Tworkov lives and works in New York and Provincetown.

Selected Exhibitions and Reviews, 1966-1981

I. Group Exhibitions

Whitney Museum of American Art, New York, *1972 Annual Exhibition: Contemporary American Painting,* January 25–March 19, 1972. Catalogue

Whitney Museum of American Art, New York, *1973 Biennial Exhibition: Contemporary American Art,* January 10–March 18, 1973. Catalogue

Whitney Museum of American Art, New York, *American Drawings 1963-1973,* May 25–July 22, 1973. Catalogue with text by Elke M. Solomon

The Cleveland Museum of Art, *Contemporary American Artists,* December 18, 1973–February 10, 1974. Catalogue with text by Tom Hinson

University Art Galleries, University of California, Santa Barbara, *Five American Painters, Recent Works: de Kooning, Mitchell, Motherwell, Resnick, Tworkov,* January 8–February 17, 1974. Catalogue with text by Phyllis Plous

University Art Gallery, State University of New York, Albany, *Tight and Loose,* January 13–February 14, 1974. Catalogue

Krannert Art Museum, Champaign-Urbana, Illinois, *Contemporary American Painting and Sculpture 1974,* March 10–April 21, 1974. Catalogue

Indianapolis Museum of Art, *Painting and Sculpture Today 1974,* May 22–July 14, 1974. Traveled to Museum of Contemporary Art, Cincinnati, September 12–October 26. Catalogue with text by Richard L. Warrum

Virginia Museum of Fine Arts, Richmond, *Twelve American Painters,* October 1-27, 1974. Catalogue

The Corcoran Gallery of Art, Washington, D.C., *The 34th Biennial of Contemporary American Painting,* February 22–April 6, 1975. Catalogue with texts by Randall De Leeuw, Linda Simmons and Roy Slade

Kennedy Art Galleries, New York, *Art Students League 100th Anniversary Show,* March 6-29, 1975. Catalogue

Grey Art Gallery, New York University, New York, *Report from Soho,* September 24–November 5, 1975

Fort Wayne Museum of Art, Indiana, *The Hue and Far Cry of Color,* May 1-30, 1976. Checklist

Hirshhorn Museum and Sculpture Garden, Smithsonian Institution, Washington, D.C., *The Golden Door: Artist-Immigrants of America, 1876-1976,* May 20–October 20, 1976. Catalogue with texts by Daniel J. Boorstin and Cynthia Jaffee McCabe

Institute of Contemporary Art, Boston, *A Selection of American Art: The Skowhegan School 1946-1976,* June 16–September 5, 1976. Catalogue with texts by Allen Ellenzweig, Lloyd Goodrich, Gabriella Jeppson, and Bernarda B. Shahn

Des Moines Art Center, *Possibilities for Collectors II,* July 6–August 15, 1976

The Solomon R. Guggenheim Museum, New York, *Acquisition Priorities: Aspects of Postwar Painting in America,* October 15, 1976–January 16, 1977

Society for Contemporary Art, The Art Institute of Chicago, *Drawings of the 70's,* March 9–May 1, 1977. Checklist

Kennedy Art Galleries, New York, *Artists Salute Skowhegan,* December 8-21, 1977

Philadelphia College of Art, *Seventies Painting,* April 21–May 21, 1978. Catalogue with text by Janet Kardon

Nancy Hoffman Gallery, New York, *Major New Works,* November 25, 1978–January 3, 1979

Century Club, New York, *Paintings and Sculpture by Artist Members of the Century Association,* January 9–February 4, 1979

The Solomon R. Guggenheim Museum, New York, *Collection: Art in America After World War II,* January 18–February 25, 1979

Century Club, New York, *Work on Paper: Murals, Watercolors, Prints, Sketches and Drawings by Artist Members,* March 6–April 1, 1979

Century Club, New York, *The New Artist Members Exhibition,* April 3–May 6, 1979

Betty Parsons Gallery, New York, *The Language of Abstraction,* June 19–August 3, 1979. Catalogue with text by Susan C. Larsen

American Academy and Institute of Arts and Letters, New York, *The Hassam and Speicher Purchase Fund Exhibition,* November 19–December 30, 1979

The Brooklyn Museum, *American Drawing in Black and White: 1970-1980,* November

22, 1980–January 18, 1981. Catalogue with text by Gene Baro

Joe and Emily Lowe Art Gallery, Syracuse University, New York, *All in Line: An Exhibition of Linear Drawing,* November 23, 1980–January 18, 1981. Catalogue with text by August Freundlich

Whitney Museum of American Art, New York, *1981 Biennial Exhibition,* January 20–April 19, 1981. Catalogue with texts by Tom Armstrong, John G. Hanhardt, Barbara Haskell, Richard Marshall and Patterson Sims

Summit Art Center, New Jersey, *Transitions,* March 6–April 1, 1981

American Academy and Institute of Arts and Letters, New York, *Exhibition of the Works of Newly Elected Members and Recipients of Awards,* May 20–June 14, 1981

Nancy Hoffman Gallery, New York, *Major New Works,* September 11–October 7, 1981

II. One-man Exhibitions and Reviews

Gertrude Kasle Gallery, Detroit, *Jack Tworkov: Monochromatic Paintings,* April 12–May 9, 1969. Checklist

Whitney Museum of American Art, New York, *Jack Tworkov: Recent Paintings,* February 5–March 14, 1971. Checklist

French & Company, New York, *Jack Tworkov,* February 13–March 10, 1971

Gertrude Kasle Gallery, Detroit, *Jack Tworkov: Recent Paintings,* November 6–December 1, 1971

French & Company, New York, *Jack Tworkov,* April 15–May 11, 1972
  K[im] L[evin], "Reviews and Previews," *Art News,* vol. 71, May 1972, p. 56
  Ellen Lubell, "In the Galleries," *Arts Magazine,* vol. 46, Summer 1972, pp. 61-62

Jaffe-Friede Gallery, Hopkins Center, Dartmouth College, Hanover, New Hampshire, *Jack Tworkov, Winter Term Artist-in-Residence,* February 9–March 4, 1973. Catalogue with text by Jack Tworkov

Nancy Hoffman Gallery, New York, *Jack Tworkov,* March 16–April 10, 1974
  Ellen Lubell, "Arts Reviews: Jack Tworkov," *Art Magazine,* vol. 48, June 1974, p. 61
  Al Brunelle, "Reviews and Previews," *Art News,* vol. 73, Summer 1974, p. 126

List Gallery, The Denver Art Museum, *Jack Tworkov: Recent Paintings,* November 30, 1974–January 5, 1975

Nancy Hoffman Gallery, New York, *Jack Tworkov,* November 8–December 4, 1975
  Ellen Lubell, "Arts Reviews," *Arts Magazine,* vol. 50, January 1976, p. 17
  Ann-Sargent Wooster, "New York Reviews," *Art News,* vol. 75, January 1976, pp. 119-120

The New Gallery, Cleveland, *Jack Tworkov: Recent Paintings and Drawings 1968-1975,* November 12–December 6, 1975. Catalogue with texts by Tom E. Hinson and Marjorie T. Talalay. Traveled to The Sullivant Gallery, Ohio State University, Columbus, January 6–February 7, 1976; Kilcawley Center Art Gallery, Youngstown State University, Ohio, February 11–March 9; The Contemporary Arts Center, Cincinnati, March 15–April 29

John Berggruen Gallery, San Francisco, *Jack Tworkov, Recent Paintings and Drawings,* April 12–May 8, 1976

University Art Galleries, University of California, Santa Barbara, *Jack Tworkov: Recent Paintings and Drawings,* January 5–February 6, 1977. Catalogue with text by Phyllis Plous

Nancy Hoffman Gallery, New York, *Jack Tworkov,* April 2–May 5, 1977
  Ellen Schwartz, "New York Reviews," *Art News,* vol. 76, Summer 1977, p. 189

Jan Baum-Iris Silverman Gallery, Los Angeles, *Jack Tworkov—The 70's Paintings and Drawings,* January 25–March 3, 1979; held concurrently with *Paintings and Drawings,* The Art Museum and Galleries, California State College, Long Beach
  Melinda Wortz, "The Nation," *Art News,* vol. 78, April 1979, p. 110

Third Eye Centre, Glasgow, *Jack Tworkov: Paintings 1950-1978,* May 18–June 17, 1979. Catalogue with texts by Dore Ashton, Richard Demarco and Andrew Forge; interview with Tworkov by Marcia Tucker. Traveled to Fruitmarket Gallery, Edinburgh, June 23–July 14; Academy Gallery, Liverpool, August 3-31; Ulster Museum, Belfast, October 4–November 4; Hatton Gallery, Newcastle-upon-Tyne, November 16–December 14

Rhode Island School of Design, Providence, *Jack Tworkov,* April 8-28, 1980

Johnson Gallery, Middlebury College, Vermont, *Jack Tworkov Paintings,* March 6-31, 1981

Selected Bibliography

This listing is primarily restricted to material published during the years covered by this exhibition. For earlier material, see *Jack Tworkov*, Whitney Museum of American Art, New York, 1964, exh. cat.

I. General

A. Books

Harold Rosenberg, *The Anxious Object: Art Today and Its Audience*, New York, 1964, pp. 50, 83

Irving Sandler, *The Triumph of American Painting: A History of Abstract Expressionism*, New York, 1970, pp. 98, 100, 219

Dore Ashton, "From the 1960's to the Present Day," *The Genius of American Painting*, John Wilmerding, ed., London, 1973, p. 332

Barbara Rose, *American Art Since 1900*, New York, 1975, pp. 125, 176-177, 234

Barbara Rose, *Readings in American Art, 1900-1975*, New York, 1975, p. 9

Sam Hunter and John Jacobus, *Modern Art from Post-Impressionism to the Present*, New York, 1976, p. 271

H. H. Arnason, *History of Modern Art*, New York, 1977, pp. 508, 525-526, 698

B. Periodicals

Barbara Rose and Irving Sandler, "Sensibility of the Sixties," *Art in America*, vol. 55, January/February 1967, pp. 44-57

Carter Ratcliff, "New York Letter," *Art International*, vol. XV, June 20, 1971, pp. 99, 105

II. On the Artist

A. Periodicals

Douglas Crimp, "Drawn and Quartered," *Art News*, vol. 70, March 1971, pp. 48-49, 72-73

Kasha Linville Gula, "Indian Summer of Jack Tworkov," *Art in America,* vol. 61, September/October 1973, pp. 62-63

April Kingsley, "Jack Tworkov," *Art International*, vol. XVIII, March 20, 1974, pp. 24-27

B. Films and Television Tapes

"Jack Tworkov," by Lane Slate, 1963

"Film on Three American Painters: Hofmann, Avery and Tworkov," produced by Warren Forma, Contemporary Films, Inc., 1963

"The New York School," produced by Michael Blackwood Productions, 1973

"Interview with Jack Tworkov," by Richard Demarco, Third Eye Centre, 1979

III. By the Artist

"Notes on My Painting," *Art in America*, vol. 61, September/October 1973, pp. 66-69

IV. Interview

Phyllis Tuchman, "An Interview with Jack Tworkov," *Artforum*, vol. IX, January 1971, pp. 62-68

Photocredits

Works in the exhibition

Color

Courtesy The Cleveland Museum of Art: cat. no. 19

Courtesy Nancy Hoffman Gallery, New York: cat. nos. 4, 18, 22, 26, 31, 34, 38, 40

Courtesy Jacob Schulman, Gloversville, New York: cat. no. 27

Black and White

Bevan Davies, New York: cat. nos. 1, 5, 9, 16, 17, 20, 21, 23-25, 28-30, 32, 35-37, 39

Phillip Galgiani, courtesy San Francisco Museum of Modern Art: cat. no. 7

Robert E. Mates: cat. no. 12

Robert E. Mates and Paul Katz: cat. nos. 3, 8, 13, 14, 15

Robert E. Mates and Paul Katz, courtesy Jacob Schulman, Gloversville, New York: cat. no. 6

Alan Zindman, New York: cat. nos. 2, 10, 11, 33, 41

Supplementary

Carmelo Guadagno: p. 14

David M. Heald: p. 59

Courtesy Nancy Hoffman Gallery, New York: fig. 1

Renate Pensold: pp. 3, 7, 17

Neil Winokur, New York: fig. 2

Exhibition 82/3

3,000 copies of this catalogue, designed by Malcolm Grear Designers, typeset by Dumar Typesetting, Inc., have been printed by Eastern Press in March 1982 for the Trustees of The Solomon R. Guggenheim Foundation on the occasion of the exhibition *Jack Tworkov: Fifteen Years of Painting*